USBORNE KEY SKILLS

Practice B

Tin

Written by
Holly Bathie

Illustrated by Magda Brol

Designed by Sharon Cooper

Series Editor: Felicity Brooks

You'll find the answer pages at the back of the book.

Here are the animals you'll meet as you work through the activities.

You can work through the activities in order, or pick and choose as you like.

Marvin

Brenda

Cody

Peck

Dilly

Bernie

Harley

What time is it?

Draw a line to join each animal to the clock he or she is talking about.

It's a quarter to three.

It's half past eleven.

It's a quarter past seven.

On the clock

Write the time on the dotted line next to each clock. One has been done for you.

.............Half past four.............

....

....

....

What time is it?

3

Draw a line to join each animal to
the clock he or she is talking about.

It's a
quarter
to two.

It's half
past twelve.

It's a quarter
past ten.

Around the clock

Continue the arrow to join up these times in order, from earliest to latest.

AM or PM?

Draw a circle around each 'am' time being described below.

My meeting is at five o'clock this afternoon.

I'm going to see a film at eleven this morning.

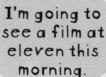

I need to be at the optician for half past three.

The food fair starts at nine this morning.

It's going to get dark around eight tonight.

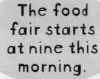

From earliest to latest

Draw a line to join up these 'am' times
in order, starting with the earliest
and finishing with the latest.

The chemist
opens at half
past eight.

I need to be at
the school at a
quarter to ten.

I'm going to
meet Suki
at a quarter
past eleven.

The bookshop
opens at a
quarter past
nine.

It's a quarter
to eight now.

What time is it?

Draw a line to join each animal to the clock he or she is talking about.

It's five thirty.

It's eleven forty-five.

It's seven fifteen.

On the clock

Write the time on the dotted
line next to each clock. One has
been done for you.

.............Twenty past two.........

....

....

....

Birthdays

Dilly and Peck both have birthdays in July. On the calendar, draw a triangle around Dilly's birthday and a ring around Peck's birthday.

My birthday is the first Saturday of the month!

Oooh, my birthday is ten days after yours.

Dilly

Peck

July

Mon	Tues	Wed	Thurs	Fri	Sat	Sun
1	2	3	4	5	6	7
8	9	10	11	12	13	14
15	16	17	18	19	20	21
22	23	24	25	26	27	28
29	30	31	1	2	3	4

Around the clock

10

Continue the arrow to join up these 'am' times in order, from the earliest to the latest time.

What time is it?

Draw a line to join each animal to
the clock he or she is talking about.

It's twenty
past eight.

It's twenty-five
past one.

It's ten past
seven.

Birthdays

Suki and Harley both have birthdays in August. On the calendar, draw a triangle around Suki's birthday and a ring around Harley's birthday.

Suki

My birthday is the last day of the month.

My birthday is two weeks before yours.

Harley

August						
Mon	Tues	Wed	Thurs	Fri	Sat	Sun
29	30	31	1	2	3	4
5	6	7	8	9	10	11
12	13	14	15	16	17	18
19	20	21	22	23	24	25
26	27	28	29	30	31	1

AM or PM?

Draw a circle around each 'pm' time being described below.

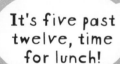

I'll meet Marvin at twenty past eight tonight.

My haircut was at twenty past nine this morning.

It's five past twelve, time for lunch!

My appointment is at ten to one this afternoon.

My meeting was at five past eleven this morning.

From earliest to latest

14

Draw a line to join up these 'pm' times
in order, starting with the earliest
and finishing with the latest.

I must catch my twelve thirty train.

I need to call the bank at ten to four.

It's due to rain at three this afternoon.

I don't want to be late for my appointment at twenty to two.

The shops will close at five forty-five today.

Brenda's day

Draw a line to join up Brenda's shopping
day in the correct order. Start with the
earliest time and finish with the latest.

Fancy Fashion

Tin Whistle

Lovely Living

Page by Page

Suki's day

Draw a line to join up Suki's shopping day in the correct order. Start with the earliest time and finish with the latest.

Brenda's party

There are three hours to go until Brenda's birthday party. It's 10am now. Draw around the clock that shows the time the party is due to start. Write that time in words on the dotted line.

Time to get decorating.

....

The fireworks display

There are two hours to go until the fireworks display. It's a quarter past seven now. Write on the dotted line the time the fireworks will start.

....

The fair is coming

The fair will arrive on the 19th of May in the morning, and leave the night of the 22nd. Circle those dates on the calendar, then write on the dotted line the length of time the fair will be in the forest for.

May

Mon	Tues	Wed	Thurs	Fri	Sat	Sun
29	30	1	2	3	4	5
6	7	8	9	10	11	12
13	14	15	16	17	18	19
20	21	22	23	24	25	26
27	28	29	30	31	1	2

....

Between dates

Lights for the fair will be put up on the
11th of May, and taken down on the 25th.
Circle those dates on the calendar, then
write on the dotted line the number of
weeks the lights will be up for.

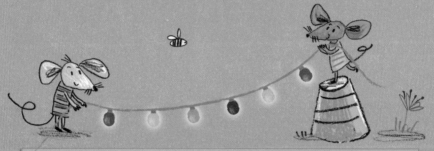

May

Mon	Tues	Wed	Thurs	Fri	Sat	Sun
29	30	1	2	3	4	5
6	7	8	9	10	11	12
13	14	15	16	17	18	19
20	21	22	23	24	25	26
27	28	29	30	31	1	2

...........................weeks

At the bike shop

On Saturdays, the bike shop opens at 9am and closes four hours later. Draw hands on the clock to show when the shop closes.

Opens

Closes

At the grocery shop

22

The grocery shop opens at half past ten and stays open for six hours. Draw hands on the clock to show when the shop closes.

Opens

Closes

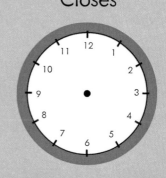

Boat to Skull Island

Read the sign, then write on the dotted lines the time each boat will reach Skull Island.

BOAT TRIPS FROM BLACK BAY TO SKULL ISLAND

•

The Nina departs at 10am
The Pinta departs at 12pm
The Santa Maria departs at 3pm

All boat trips last one and a half hours.

The Nina ....

The Pinta ....

The Santa Maria ....

Return journey

Read the sign, then write on the dotted lines the time each boat will return to Black Bay.

BOAT TRIPS FROM SKULL ISLAND TO BLACK BAY

•

The Nina departs at 12pm
The Pinta departs at 2pm
The Santa Maria departs at 5pm

All boat trips last one and a half hours.

The Nina ....

The Pinta ....

The Santa Maria ....

Suki's gardening

It's a quarter to six. Suki started gardening
four hours ago. Circle the clock that
shows the time she started. Write that
time in words on the dotted line.

Phew! Nearly time to stop.

....

At the post office

It's 4pm and the post office is closing now. It has been open for five and a half hours. Draw hands on the clock to show when the post office opened.

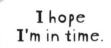

Opens

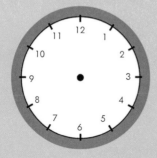

Closes

Bernie's baking

It's a quarter to four. Bernie has been busy baking for three hours. Circle the clock that shows the time he started. Write that time in words on the dotted line.

....

At the art gallery

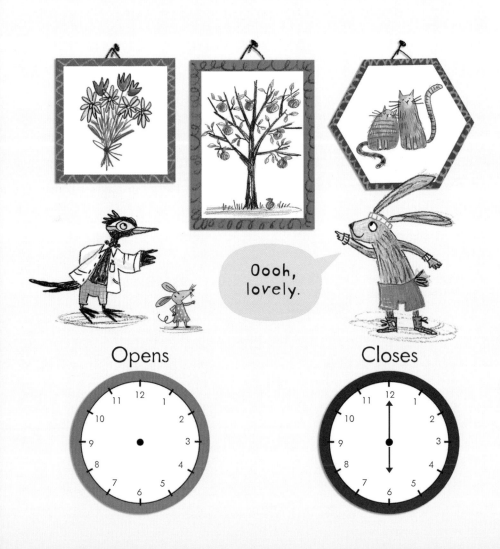

It's 6pm and the art gallery is closing now.
It has been open for eight and a half hours.
Draw hands on the clock to show when it opened.

Oooh, lovely.

Opens

Closes

Minutes past

Write the time in words on the dotted
line underneath each clock.

...................minutes past...................

...................minutes past...................

Matching times

Each clock is being described by two
mice. Draw lines to join the correct
two mice to each one.

It's twelve
fifteen.

It's a
quarter to
eleven.

It's ten
forty-five.

It's nine
thirty.

It's half
past nine.

It's a
quarter past
twelve.

Minutes past

Write the time in words on the dotted
line underneath each clock.

..................minutes past...................

..................minutes past...................

Matching times

Each clock is being described by two
mice. Draw lines to join the correct
two mice to each one.

Running late

These friends were due to meet for lunch at a quarter past twelve. Draw the hands on the clocks to show when each of them will arrive.

It's a quarter past twelve now. Where are the others?

Sorry, I'm going to be another twenty-five minutes...

I'll be there in fifteen minutes!

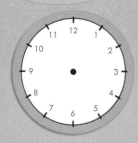

I'm five minutes away!

Arriving early

Arriving early

Art class starts at 1pm and these animals have all arrived early. Draw the time on the clocks to show when each of them arrived.

I'm ten minutes early.

Marvin

Peck

I got here ten minutes before you, Marvin.

I got here five minutes before you, Peck.

You can all come in now!

Cody

Minutes past

Write the time in words on the
dotted line underneath each clock.

...............................minutes past.........................

...............................minutes past.........................

What time is it?

36

Draw a line to join each animal to the clock he or she is talking about.

It's twenty past ten.

It's ten to twelve.

It's five to four.

The circus is coming

Harley needs to put up posters the Saturday
before the circus arrives. Draw a circle
around the date he needs to put up posters.

The circus is
going to be
great!

CIRCUS

13th April

April						
Mon	Tues	Wed	Thurs	Fri	Sat	Sun
1	2	3	4	5	6	7
8	9	10	11	12	13	14
15	16	17	18	19	20	21
22	23	24	25	26	27	28
29	30	1	2	3	4	5

A date to remember

Cody will arrange for the bunting to be taken down ten days after the circus leaves. Draw a triangle around the date Cody needs to remember.

April						
Mon	Tues	Wed	Thurs	Fri	Sat	Sun
1	2	3	4	5	6	7
8	9	10	11	12	13	14
15	16	17	18	19	20 Circus leaves!	21
22	23	24	25	26	27	28
29	30	1	2	3	4	5

Minutes past

Write the time in words on the
dotted line underneath each clock.

.............................minutes past..........................

.............................minutes past..........................

What time is it?

40

Draw a line to join each animal to the clock he or she is talking about.

It's twenty to eleven.

It's ten past six.

It's five to two.

Peck's skating lesson

41

Peck's ice skating lesson is forty minutes long and starts at 9:45. Draw the hands on the clocks to show when her lesson starts and finishes.

You've got the hang of it, Peck!

Starts

Finishes

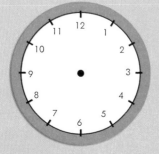

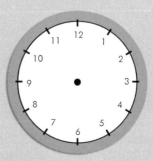

Brenda's skating lesson

Brenda's ice skating lesson is fifty minutes long and starts at 10:20. Draw the hands on the clocks to show when her lesson starts and finishes.

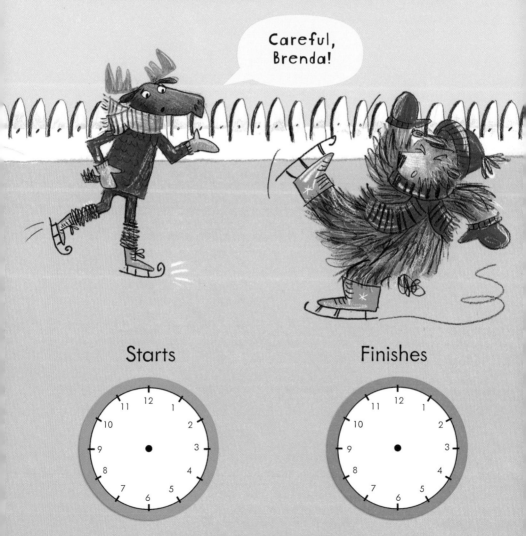

Careful, Brenda!

Starts

Finishes

Running late

These friends were supposed to meet for tea and cake at four twenty. Draw the hands on the clocks to show when each of them will arrive.

It's twenty past four now. Where are the others?

Sorry, I'm going to be twenty-five minutes late...

I'll be there in fifteen minutes!

I'm five minutes away!

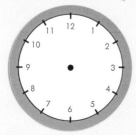

Arriving early

Writing class starts at 3:30pm and these animals have all arrived early. Draw the time on the clocks to show when each of them arrived.

Camping trip

The animals arrived at camp the morning of the 11th of July. They will leave the evening of the 17th. Circle those dates on the calendar and write the duration of the camping trip in days on the dotted line.

July

Mon	Tues	Wed	Thurs	Fri	Sat	Sun
1	2	3	4	5	6	7
8	9	10	11	12	13	14
15	16	17	18	19	20	21
22	23	24	25	26	27	28
29	30	31	1	2	3	4

Lots of snow

It started to snow in the forest on the 23rd of January and stopped snowing the morning of the 30th. Circle those dates on the calendar, then write on the dotted line the length of time it snowed for in weeks.

January						
Mon	Tues	Wed	Thurs	Fri	Sat	Sun
31	1	2	3	4	5	6
7	8	9	10	11	12	13
14	15	16	17	18	19	20
21	22	23	24	25	26	27
28	29	30	31	1	2	3

....

Skateboarding

Draw the hands on the clocks to
show the time the skateboarding
competition starts and finishes.

• SKATECHAMP •
30 minutes
of drops, flips
and dips.
Don't miss
this competition!

START TIME 5:10PM

Starts

Finishes

Football match

Draw the hands on the clocks
to show when the football
match starts and finishes.

- The-
Hoptown Hares

vs

- The-
Cunning Coyotes

Start time 11:30am
45 minute match

Starts

Finishes

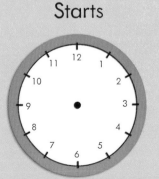

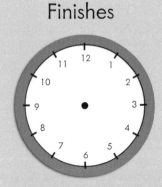

Plane to Mouse Island

Read the sign, then write on the dotted lines the time each plane will arrive at Mouse Island.

PLANE RIDES FROM CUTHBERT'S CLIFF TO MOUSE ISLAND

•

The Whistler departs at 9am
Seadart departs at 11:30am
Captain Cloud departs at 4:15pm

All plane rides last 45 minutes.

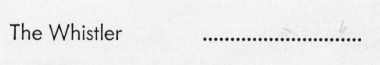

The Whistler ....

Seadart ....

Captain Cloud ....

Return journey

Read the sign, then write on the dotted lines the time each plane will arrive at Cuthbert's Cliff.

> ## PLANE RIDES FROM MOUSE ISLAND TO CUTHBERT'S CLIFF
>
> •
>
> The Whistler departs at 10:15am
> Seadart departs at 1:45pm
> Captain Cloud departs at 5:30pm
>
> All plane rides last 45 minutes.

The Whistler ....

Seadart ....

Captain Cloud ....

Minutes past

Write the time in words on the dotted
line underneath each clock.

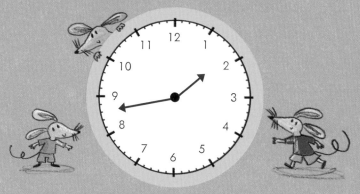

..................................minutes past..........................

..................................minutes past..........................

At the dentist

Suki needs to see the dentist. Her appointment is at two thirty. Show that time on the blank clock, then write on the dotted line the number of minutes she has to wait until her appointment.

Dentist

......................minutes

Minutes past

Write the time in words on the dotted
line underneath each clock.

..........................minutes past.......................

.........................minutes past.....................

At the hairdresser

Peck's haircut is at twenty past eleven.
Show that time on the blank clock, then write
on the dotted line the number of minutes she
has to wait until her appointment.

..........................minutes

Minutes past

Write the time in words on the dotted
line underneath each clock.

...........................minutes past........................

...........................minutes past........................

The weather in March

Dilly's reading the weather forecast for March.
Circle all the sunny days on the calendar.
Now write on the dotted line the length of
time it will be sunny for, in weeks and days.

From the **12th**
of **March** it will
be sunny every
day for ten days
in a row.

			March			
Mon	Tues	Wed	Thurs	Fri	Sat	Sun
25	26	27	28	1	2	3
4	5	6	7	8	9	10
11	12	13	14	15	16	17
18	19	20	21	22	23	24
25	26	27	28	29	30	31

...................week(s) and...................days

Minutes past

Write the time in words on the dotted
line underneath each clock.

.....................................minutes past.........................

.............................minutes past.........................

The weather in April

Dilly's reading the weather forecast for April.
Circle all the cloudy days on the calendar.
Now write on the dotted line the length
of time it will be cloudy for, in days.

From the **12th**
to the 27th
we can expect
solid cloud.

April						
Mon	Tues	Wed	Thurs	Fri	Sat	Sun
1	2	3	4	5	6	7
8	9	10	11	12	13	14
15	16	17	18	19	20	21
22	23	24	25	26	27	28
29	30	1	2	3	4	5

...................days

Waiting for the bus

The mice's bus is due at eight fifty-six.
Show that time on the blank clock, then
write on the dotted line the number of
minutes the mice have to wait for their bus.

It won't be
long now!

..........................minutes

Waiting for the train

Cody's train has been delayed. It's now due at seven forty-two. Show that time on the blank clock, then write on the dotted line the number of minutes he has to wait until it arrives.

...................minutes

On the phone

Brenda called Bernie at five forty-five and they're still talking. Write on the dotted line the length of time they have been on the phone for.

..........................minutes

Windy days

This month these friends flew their kites every day from the 3rd to the 11th. Circle each day of kite-flying on the calendar, then write on the dotted line the number of weeks and days they flew their kites for.

June

Mon	Tues	Wed	Thurs	Fri	Sat	Sun
27	28	29	30	31	1	2
3	4	5	6	7	8	9
10	11	12	13	14	15	16
17	18	19	20	21	22	23
24	25	26	27	28	29	30

...................week(s) and...................days

Wrapping presents

Suki started wrapping presents at eight twenty-five. Write on the dotted line the number of minutes she has been wrapping presents for.

Marvin will love this.

.....................minutes

Lots of rain

In February it rained every day from the 19th to the 28th. Circle those two dates on the calendar, then write on the dotted line the number of days it rained for.

February						
Mon	Tues	Wed	Thurs	Fri	Sat	Sun
28	29	30	31	1	2	3
4	5	6	7	8	9	10
11	12	13	14	15	16	17
18	19	20	21	22	23	24
25	26	27	28	1	2	3

....

What time is it?

Draw lines to join each analogue
clock to the matching digital clock.

65

11 : 45

02 : 15

05 : 30

On the clock

Write the time on the dotted line next to each clock. One has been done for you.

04:30 ....Half past four.....

10:15 ....

07:00 ....

12:45

....

What time is it?

Draw lines to join each digital clock
to the matching analogue clock.

On the clock

Write the time on the dotted line next to each clock. One has been done for you.

02:40 ......Twenty to three......

12:05 ....

05:45 ....

11:10 ....

Marvin's train

This analogue clock shows the time now. Marvin's train will arrive soon. Write the 'pm' time on the digital display board to show when it will arrive.

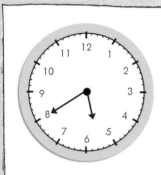

1st. LONE TREE PLAIN
Calling at: Hopping Common, Fir View and Lone Tree Plain.

Arrives at ....:............

My train will arrive in fifteen minutes.

Departure times

Draw the hands on the analogue clocks to show when each animal's train will depart.

1st. Fir Town *Calling at: Fir Town only.*

2nd. Pine View *Calling at: Cedar Grove and Pine View.*

TIME NOW 12 : 10

My train departs in twelve minutes.

My train won't leave for another five minutes.

Kite flying

It's 16:30 and these friends started flying
their kites forty-five minutes ago. Circle the
clock that shows when they started.

15:30   15:45   15:05

Running

It's 11:05 and Harley and Cody started running forty minutes ago. Circle the clock that shows when they started running.

10:45   10:25   10:10

AM or PM?

Draw a circle around
each 'am' time below.

14:07

05:11

23:09

19:25

10:43

06:19

From earliest to latest

Draw a line to join up these 'am' times
in order, starting with the earliest
and finishing with the latest.

11 : 30

07 : 55

05 : 20

10 : 35

10 : 50

09 : 40

AM or PM?

Draw a circle around
each 'pm' time below.

07 : 19

20 : 54

17 : 09

23 : 59

00 : 04

11 : 16

From earliest to latest

Draw a line to join up these 'pm'
times in order, starting with the
earliest and finishing with the latest.

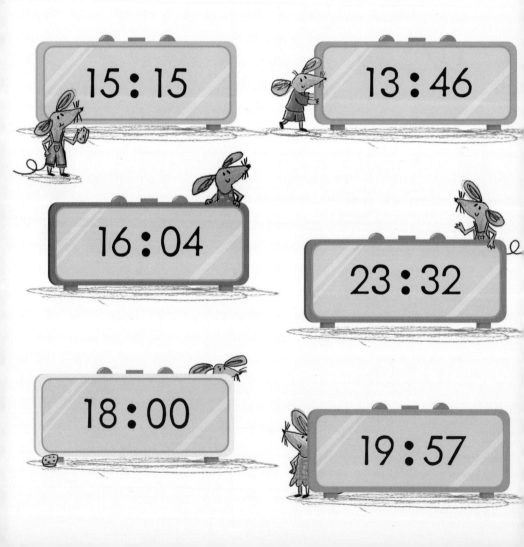

15:15

13:46

16:04

23:32

18:00

19:57

Harley's day

Draw a line to join up Harley's day
in the correct order. Start with the
earliest time and finish with the latest.

12:40

11:00

15:50

09:25

Bernie's day

Draw a line to join up Bernie's day in the correct order. Start with the earliest time and finish with the latest.

08:57

11:11

20:23

14:40

78

Story writing

It's the morning of the 8th of May and Harley is writing a story for a magazine. He has ten days left to finish it before the magazine is printed. Draw a circle around the date it will be printed.

...and then a genie appeared!

May						
Mon	Tues	Wed	Thurs	Fri	Sat	Sun
29	30	1	2	3	4	5
6	7	8	9	10	11	12
13	14	15	16	17	18	19
20	21	22	23	24	25	26
27	28	29	30	31	1	2

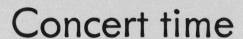

Concert time

It's the 6th of October. Dilly and Bernie
cannot wait for the Super Skunks concert.
Circle the date of the concert on the calendar,
then write how many weeks are left to go.

October						
Mon	Tues	Wed	Thurs	Fri	Sat	Sun
31	1	2	3	4	5	6
7	8	9	10	11	12	13
14	15	16	17	18	19	20
21	22	23	24	25	26	27
28	29	30	31	1	2	3

....................weeks

Basketball game

Marvin's basketball game started at 7pm.
Fill in the digital clocks to show
when the game started and finished.

Started

Finished

Hours and minutes

The duration of each TV programme is given in minutes. Write the duration of each programme in hours and minutes on the dotted lines.

Channel 20

Tree Rescue

12:30

102 minutes

....

Channel 3

Did You Know?

13:00

88 minutes

....

Time for a film

Suki's film is starting. It is 92 minutes
long. Draw and write the time it
will finish on the clocks below.

Two Flew into the Owl's Nest

Start

16:10

Finish

Minutes only

The duration of each TV programme is given in hours and minutes. Write on the dotted lines the duration of each programme in minutes only.

Channel 6

Mouse Masterclass

14:30

1 hour and 15 minutes

....

Channel 43

Leaf Watch

18:10

1 hour and 55 minutes

....

What time is it?

Draw lines to join each analogue clock to the matching digital time.

18 : 16

13 : 48

10 : 34

Years and months

These friends know how old their trees are in months only. Write on the dotted lines how old their trees are in years and months.

> My tree is twenty-six months old.

....

> My tree is fourteen months old.

....

Bus timetable

Dilly and Peck's bus departs at 15:40.
On the timetable, draw a ring around
the time they will arrive at Cabin Lodge.

I'm so tired from our hike.

We can put our feet up at Cabin Lodge!

Windy Creek

Route 71 – Raccoon Ranch to Firtown						
	Monday-Saturday				Sundays	
Raccoon Ranch	0730	1120	1505	1542	1003	1749
Windy Creek	|	1155	1540	1617	1038	|
Long River	0825	1215	1620	1737	1058	|
Cabin Lodge	|	1307	1708	2025	1146	1909
Firtown	0845	1242	1713	2030	1151	1914

Journey duration

Complete the other side of this page. Now, write the duration of Dilly and Peck's bus journey on the dotted line in hours and minutes.

What time is it?

Draw lines to join each analogue
clock to the matching digital time.

04:45

07:27

11:09

Months only

These friends know how old their trees are in years and months. Write on the dotted lines how old their trees are in months only.

My tree is three years and one month old.

....

My tree is one year and ten months old.

....

Brenda's train

This analogue clock shows the time now. Brenda's train will arrive soon. Write the 'pm' time on the digital display board to show when it will arrive.

1st. RACCOON RANCH
Calling at: Windy Creek, and Raccoon Ranch.

Arrives at ....:............

I've got ten minutes until my train arrives.

Departure times

Draw the hands on the analogue clocks to show when each animal's train will depart.

> 1st. Windy Creek *Calling at: Hawthorn Hill and Windy Creek.*
>
> 2nd. Long River *Calling at: Long River only.*
>
> TIME NOW 17 : 50

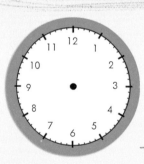

My train departs in twelve minutes.

My train won't leave for another five minutes.

Matching times

The animals know the duration of their journeys. Draw a line to match each animal to the correct departure board.

My journey will be an hour and five minutes.

FIRTOWN
Departs at 07:19
Arrives at   07:36

My journey will be seventeen minutes.

CABIN LODGE
Departs at 16:02
Arrives at   16:57

My journey will be fifty-five minutes.

LONG RIVER
Departs at 13:15
Arrives at   14:20

Dilly's baking

Help Dilly follow her cake recipe this afternoon.
Look at the analogue clock, then write the time
on the digital clock after each step.

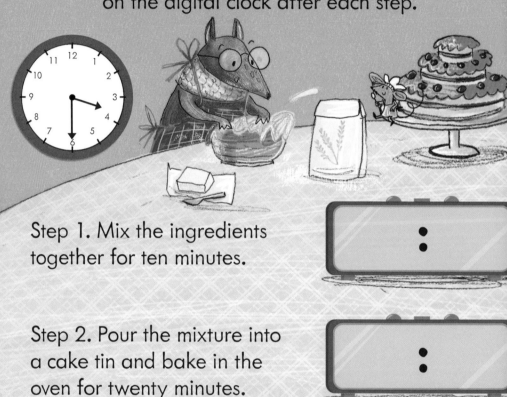

Step 1. Mix the ingredients
together for ten minutes.

Step 2. Pour the mixture into
a cake tin and bake in the
oven for twenty minutes.

Step 3. Take out the
cake and leave to cool
for fifteen minutes.

Bernie's baking

Bernie is making a flan for lunch.
Look at the analogue clock, then write the
time on the digital clock after each step.

Step 1. Roll out a circle of
pastry and place in a flan tin.
This will only take five minutes.

Step 2. Mix the ingredients
together for ten minutes
until smooth.

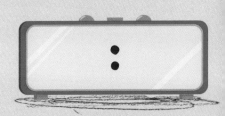

Step 3. Pour the mixture over
the pastry and bake in the
oven for twenty-five minutes.

Matching times

The animals know the duration of their journeys. Draw a line to match each animal to the correct train.

FIR VIEW

Departs at 11:15
Arrives at 13:45

My journey will be an hour and twenty minutes.

WINDY CREEK

Departs at 15:25
Arrives at 15:50

My journey will be twenty-five minutes.

My journey will be two and a half hours.

RACCOON RANCH

Departs at 09:15
Arrives at 10:35

Bus timetable

It's four o'clock on Tuesday and Suki and Cody need to be in Firtown by 6pm for Brenda's party. Draw a ring around the time they need to get the bus.

I hope we get there in time for the party.

Route 71 – Raccoon Ranch to Firtown						
	Monday-Saturday				Sundays	
Raccoon Ranch	0730	1120	1505	1542	1003	1749
Windy Creek		1155	1540	1617	1038	
Long River	0825	1215	1620	1737	1058	
Cabin Lodge		1307	1708	2025	1146	1909
Firtown	0845	1242	1713	2030	1151	1914

Journey duration

Complete the other side of this page.
Now, write the duration of Cody and
Suki's bus journey on the dotted line.

Path laying

It's the 2nd of October. Harley and Suki are laying a new path in the park. It needs to be finished in three weeks. Draw a ring around the deadline date.

We need to finish the path in time for the music festival.

October						
Mon	Tues	Wed	Thurs	Fri	Sat	Sun
30	1	2	3	4	5	6
7	8	9	10	11	12	13
14	15	16	17	18	19	20
21	22	23	24	25	26	27
28	29	30	31	1	2	3

Holiday time

It's the 15th of August. Dilly is going on holiday in four days' time and needs to pack. Draw a ring around the date she goes on holiday.

Oh I can't decide!

August						
Mon	Tues	Wed	Thurs	Fri	Sat	Sun
29	30	31	1	2	3	4
5	6	7	8	9	10	11
12	13	14	15	16	17	18
19	20	21	22	23	24	25
26	27	28	29	30	31	1

TV schedule

How long is each TV programme?
Draw lines to join up the
programmes with their descriptions.

Forest Falls
18:15 — 18:45

An hour and a half
of non-stop action.
Don't miss it!

The High Life
20:05 — 21:35

You'll be gripped by
this fast-paced drama
series; each episode
is only 40 minutes.

WOODLANDERS
21:00 — 21:40

Prepare for giggles
galore in this half hour
special from your
favourite comedian.

Skating festival

It's the ice skating festival today.
Write the duration of each
event on the dotted lines.

Speed skating competition

13 : 20 – 13 : 50

....

Partner dancing

14 : 05 – 14 : 35

....

Freestyle skate

15 : 10 – 15 : 30

....

Film times

Draw arrows to join up the starting times
of the films in the correct order. Begin with
the earliest time and finish with the latest.

Ballet Bears	08:20	13:00
Moose on the Loose	14:05	18:30
Autumn Days	10:45	11:30
River Rescue: Part 2	16:10	19:55

Film duration

Draw a line to join up the durations of the animals' films in the correct order. Start with the shortest film and finish with the longest.

My film was two hours.

My film was an hour and twenty minutes.

My film was an hour and ten minutes.

My film was 90 minutes.

Film times

Draw arrows to join up the starting times
of the films in the correct order. Begin with
the earliest time and finish with the latest.

Armadillo in New York	12:05	21:40
Broken Branches	11:10	13:35
The Quiet Road	13:25	20:50
The Secret Forest	09:30	15:00

Film duration

Draw a line to join up the durations of the animals' films in the correct order. Start with the longest film and finish with the shortest.

TV schedule

How long is each TV programme?
Draw lines to join up the programmes
with their descriptions.

Did the butler do it?
All will be revealed in
tonight's 75 minute finale.

MAKE OR BREAK
10:35 — 12:35

At two hours long,
this overblown caper
drags. Give it a miss.

TURF WARS
12:20 — 13:10

Settle on the sofa
for the funniest fifty
minutes of your week.

IN THE TREEHOUSE
17:30 — 18:45

Swimming gala

It's the swimming gala today.
Write the duration of each event
on the dotted lines.

100 METRES FRONT CRAWL

09 : 40 – 09 : 50

....

TREADING WATER

10 : 15 – 10 : 20

....

HIGH DIVE

11 : 45 – 12 : 10

....

Hours and minutes

These friends have spent 80 minutes fishing. Write on the dotted line the length of time they have been fishing for in hours and minutes.

I've found some tiny fish!

I can see a few more, Marvin.

....

Matching times

110

Draw a line to match up each pair of animals who are talking about the same length of time.

I've got twenty minutes to read my script.

I've got thirty minutes until the play starts.

I need to be ready in fifteen minutes!

I've got five minutes longer than you.

The play starts in half an hour.

I've only got half that time to get ready!

Minutes only

The Super Skunks have been playing for three hours and seven minutes. Write on the dotted line the length of time they have been playing for in minutes only.

Matching times

Draw a line to match up each pair of animals
who are talking about the same length of time.

My dental
appointment
is in ten
minutes.

I've been
waiting
twice that
long!

Phew, twenty
minutes – that
wasn't too
long.

Don't eat or
drink for a
quarter of
an hour.

I've been here
for fifteen
minutes.

I 've been her
five minutes
less than that

Years and months

These friends know how old their trees are in months only. Write on the dotted lines how old their trees are in years and months.

My tree is twenty eight months old.

....

My tree is seventeen months old.

....

Months only

These friends know how old their trees are in years and months. Write on the dotted lines how old their trees are in months only.

My tree is a year and nine months old.

My tree is just a year old.

Film times

Draw arrows to join up the starting times
of the films in the correct order. Begin with
the earliest time and finish with the latest.

Underground	21:25	22:15
The Dambuilders	12:35	13:15
Hare and There	11:05	15:45
The Coyote Kid	08:50	10:10

Film duration

Draw a line to join up the durations of the animals' films in the correct order. Start with the shortest film and finish with the longest.

My film was **100** minutes long.

Mine was half as long as that.

My film was an hour and a half.

Mine was twice as long as yours!

116

Dilly's baking

Dilly is making a cake again this afternoon.
Look at the analogue clock, then write the time
on the digital clock after each step of the recipe.

Step 1. Mix the ingredients together for fifteen minutes.

Step 2. Pour the mixture into a cake tin and bake in the oven for thirty-five minutes.

Step 3. Take out the out and leave to cool for twenty minutes.

Bernie's baking

Bernie is making a pie this morning. Look at the analogue clock, then write the time on the digital clock after each step of the recipe.

Step 1. Roll out two pastry circles and place one in a pie dish. This will take ten minutes.

Step 2. Make the pie filling and put in the pie dish. This will take twenty-five minutes.

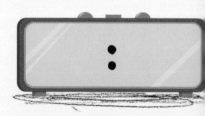

Step 3. Put the second pastry circle on top and bake in the oven for thirty minutes.

Matching times

Each clock is being described by two
mice. Draw lines to join the correct
two mice to each one.

It's five
fifteen.

It's seven
minutes to
five.

17 : 15

It's four
fifty-three.

It's a
quarter to
two.

13 : 45

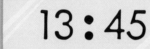

It's one
forty-five.

It's a
quarter
past five.

04 : 53

Dilly's bus

Dilly is waiting for a bus. She is due to arrive in Firtown at a quarter to nine. Draw a ring around the time of the bus she is waiting for.

Route 71 – Raccoon Ranch to Firtown						
	Monday-Saturday				Sundays	
Raccoon Ranch	0730	1120	1505	1542	1003	1749
Windy Creek	|	1155	1540	1617	1038	|
Long River	0825	1215	1620	1737	1058	|
Cabin Lodge	|	1307	1708	2025	1146	1909
Firtown	0845	1242	1713	2030	1151	1914

Marvin's bus

It's three o'clock on Friday and Marvin wants to get to Long River before the shops close at half past five. Draw a ring around the time he needs to catch the bus.

I need a new hat!

Raccoon Ranch

Route 71 – Raccoon Ranch to Firtown						
	Monday-Saturday				Sundays	
Raccoon Ranch	0730	1120	1505	1542	1003	1749
Windy Creek	|	1155	1540	1617	1038	|
Long River	0825	1215	1620	1737	1058	|
Cabin Lodge	|	1307	1708	2025	1146	1909
Firtown	0845	1242	1713	2030	1151	1914

Matching times

122

Each clock is being described by two
mice. Draw lines to join the correct
two mice to each one.

It's half
past three.

It's eight
twenty-five.

23 : 20

It's eleven
twenty.

It's twenty
past eleven.

20 : 25

It's
twenty-five
past eight.

It's three
thirty.

15 : 30

The pirate play

The pirate play is starting. The interval will be at eight fifteen. Show that time on the blank clock, then write on the dotted line how long it is until the interval.

19 : 35

:

Sail Away!
by Marvin

Captain Bessie
played by Brenda

Despicable Sue
played by Dilly

Pirate Paul
played by Bernie

......................minutes

Interval

The interval is over and the play is about to start again. It will finish at nine thirty. Show that time on the blank clock, then write on the dotted line how long it is until the play finishes.

Sail Away!

by Marvin

Pirate Joe
played by Cody

Sailor Sal
played by Suki

Pirate Pete
played by Peck

.......................minutes

A rainy day

It's due to stop raining today at 2pm. Write that time on the blank clock, then write on the dotted lines the number of hours and minutes Brenda and Bernie have to wait until it stops raining.

..............hours and..............minutes.

Waiting for the ferry

Brenda and Bernie's ferry is delayed until five past five. Write on the dotted line the number of minutes Brenda and Bernie will have to wait for their ferry.

16 : 24

..................minutes

Hours and minutes

The duration of each TV programme is given in minutes. Write on the dotted lines the duration of each programme in hours and minutes.

Channel 17

TREASURE HUNT

193 minutes

....

Channel 2

SING WITH SUKI

65 minutes

....

Minutes only

The duration of each TV programme is given in hours and minutes. Write on the dotted lines the duration of each programme in minutes only.

Channel 23

DO IT YOURSELF

2 hours and 10 minutes

....

Channel 30

CAR CHAT

1 hour and 40 minutes

....

Stopwatch times

These animals have completed their sports day races in less than an hour. Write their times on the blank stopwatches below.

We finished in twenty minutes and twenty-six seconds.

I finished in fifty eight seconds!

00 :   :

00 :   :

Ordering results

These animals have finished the
morning fun run. Write in the boxes
the order the animals finished the
fun run in, from 1st to 4th.

00 : 46 : 10

01 : 30 : 57

01 : 57 : 35

00 : 23 : 06

Timing

Suki is timing Brenda doing her homework. Write her time on the blank stopwatch below.

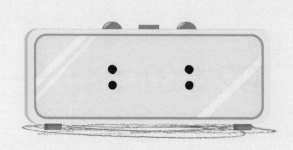

Ordering results

These animals have finished the afternoon fun run. Write in the boxes the order the animals finished the fun run in, from 1st to 4th.

02 : 31 : 45

02 : 17 : 03

01 : 08 : 29

01 : 48 : 45

Stopwatch times

These animals have completed their sports day races. Write their times on the blank stopwatches below.

I finished in seven minutes and seventeen seconds.

We finished in eleven minutes and thirty nine seconds.

00:    :

00:    :

Timing

Suki is timing how long Harley can keep his kite in the air for. Write his time so far on the blank stopwatch below.

Timing

It's a stormy day and Suki is timing how long it is after seeing the lightning that she and Dilly hear the thunderclap. Write the time they have recorded on the blank stopwatch below.

Practice page

Practice page

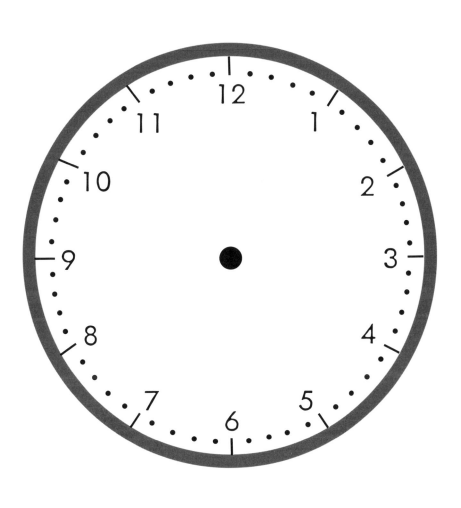

It is [ ] : [ ] am It is [ ] : [ ] pm

Practice page

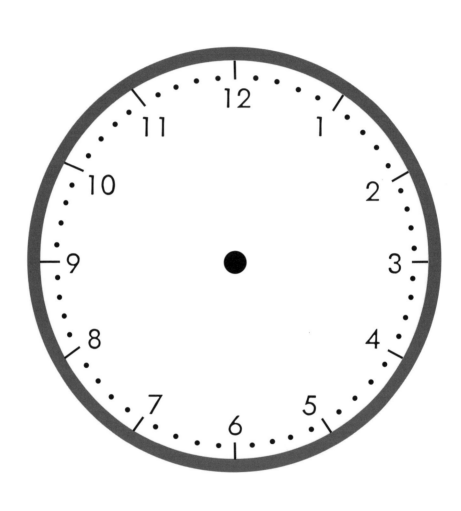

It is ▢ : ▢ am   It is ▢ : ▢ pm

Practice page

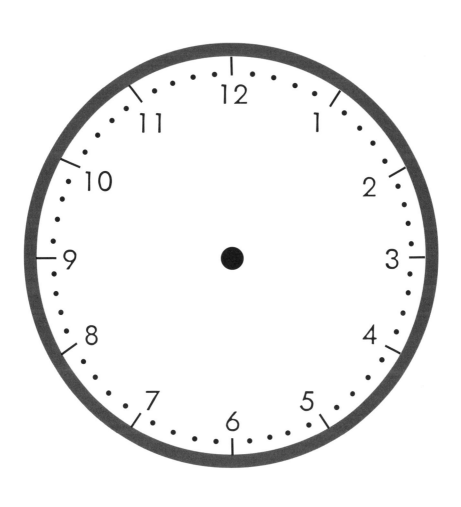

It is [ ] : [ ] am   It is [ ] : [ ] pm

Practice page

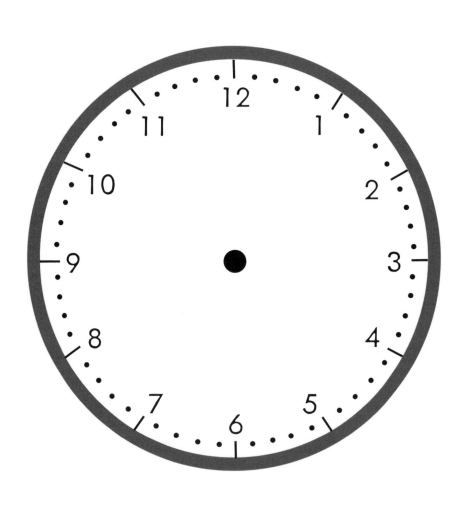

It is [ ] : [ ] am   It is [ ] : [ ] pm

Practice page

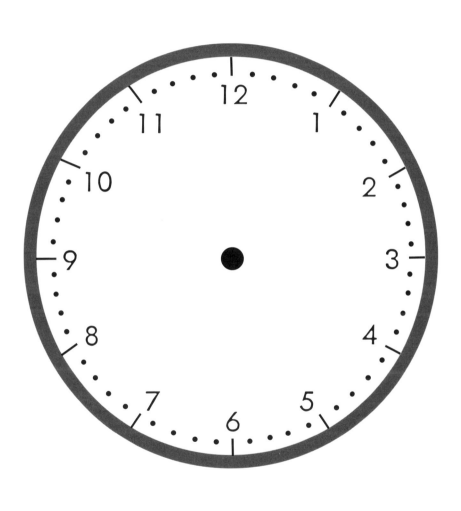

It is [ ] : [ ] am   It is [ ] : [ ] pm

Practice page

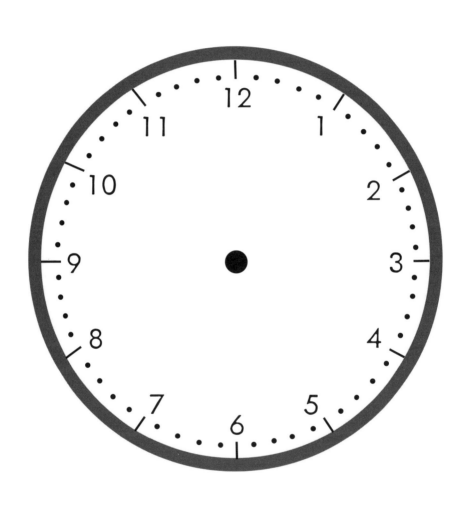

It is [ ] : [ ] am   It is [ ] : [ ] pm

Practice page

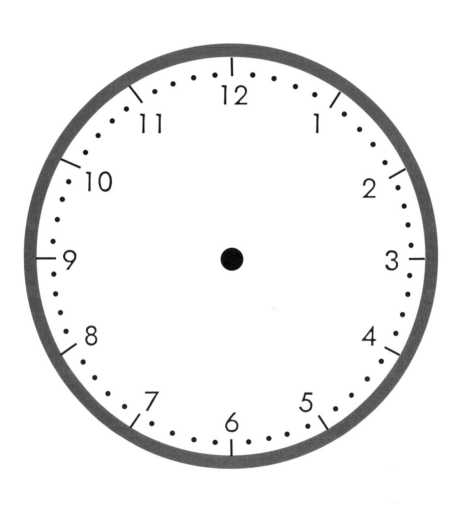

It is [ ] : [ ] am   It is [ ] : [ ] pm

Answers

What time is it? — 1

Draw a line to join each animal to the clock he or she is talking about.

On the clock — 2

Write the time on the dotted line next to each clock. One has been done for you.

Half past four

Six o'clock

A quarter past one

A quarter to eight

What time is it? — 3

Draw a line to join each animal to the clock he or she is talking about.

Around the clock — 4

Continue the arrow to join up these times in order, from earliest to latest.

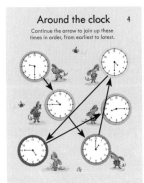

AM or PM? — 5

Draw a circle around each 'am' time being described below.

From earliest to latest — 6

Draw a line to join up these 'am' times in order, starting with the earliest and finishing with the latest.

What time is it? — 7

Draw a line to join each animal to the clock he or she is talking about.

On the clock — 8

Write the time on the dotted line next to each clock. One has been done for you.

Twenty past two

Ten to six

Five past eleven

Twenty-five to five

Birthdays — 9

Dilly and Peck both have birthdays in July. On the calendar, draw a triangle around Dilly's birthday and a ring around Peck's birthday.

Answers

Around the clock 10

Continue the arrow to join up these 'am' times in order, from the earliest to the latest time.

What time is it? 11

Draw a line to join each animal to the clock he or she is talking about.

It's twenty past eight.

It's twenty-five past one.

It's ten past seven.

Birthdays 12

Suki and Harley both have birthdays in August. On the calendar, draw a triangle around Suki's birthday and a ring around Harley's birthday.

My birthday is the last day of the month.

My birthday is two weeks before yours.

AM or PM? 13

Draw a circle around each 'pm' time being described below.

I'll meet Marvin at twenty past eight tonight.

My haircut was at twenty past nine this morning.

It's five past twelve, time for lunch!

My appointment is at ten to one this afternoon.

My meeting was at five past eleven this morning.

From earliest to latest 14

Draw lines to join up these 'pm' times in order, starting with the earliest and finishing with the latest.

I must catch my twelve thirty train.

I need to call the bank at ten to four.

It's due to rain at three this afternoon.

I don't want to be late for my appointment at twenty to two.

The shops will close at five forty-five today.

Brenda's day 15

Draw a line to join up Brenda's shopping day in the correct order. Start with the earliest time and finish with the latest.

Fancy Fashion

Tin Whistle

Lovely Living

Page by Page

Suki's day 16

Draw a line to join up Suki's shopping day in the correct order. Start with the earliest time and finish with the latest.

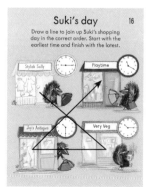

Stylish Sally

Playtime

Joy's Antiques

Very Veg

Brenda's party 17

There are three hours to go until Brenda's birthday party. It's 10am now. Draw around the clock that shows the time the party is due to start. Write that time in words on the dotted line.

Time to get decorating

...............1pm, or one o'clock...........

The fireworks display 18

There are two hours to go until the fireworks display. It's a quarter past seven now. Write on the dotted line the time the fireworks will start.

I love fireworks. I can't wait!

FIREWORKS TONIGHT!

...............A quarter past nine...........

Answers

The fair is coming   19

The fair will arrive on the 19th of May in the morning, and leave the night of the 22nd. Circle those dates on the calendar, then write on the dotted line the length of time the fair will be in the forest for.

4 days

Between dates   20

Lights for the fair will be put up on the 11th of May, and taken down on the 25th. Circle those dates on the calendar, then write on the dotted line the number of weeks the lights will be up for.

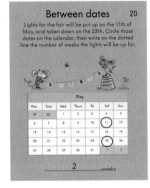

2 weeks

At the bike shop   21

On Saturdays, the bike shop opens at 9am and closes four hours later. Draw hands on the clock to show when the shop closes.

At the grocery shop   22

The grocery shop opens at half past ten and stays open for six hours. Draw hands on the clock to show when the grocery shop closes.

Boat to Skull Island   23

Read the sign, then write on the dotted lines the time each boat will reach Skull Island.

The Nina   11:30am
The Pinta   1:30pm
The Santa Maria 4:30pm

Return journey   24

Read the sign, then write on the dotted lines the time each boat will reach Black Bay.

The Nina   1:30pm
The Pinta   3:30pm
The Santa Maria 6:30pm

Suki's gardening   25

It's a quarter to six. Suki started gardening four hours ago. Circle the clock that shows the time she started. Write that time in words on the dotted line.

A quarter to two

At the post office   26

It's 4pm and the post office is closing now. It has been open for five and a half hours. Draw hands on the clock to show when the post office opened.

Bernie's baking   27

It's a quarter to four. Bernie has been busy baking for three hours. Circle the clock that shows the time he started. Write that time in words on the dotted line.

A quarter to one

Answers

At the art gallery 28

It's 6pm and the art gallery is closing now.
It has been open for eight and a half hours.
Draw hands on the clock to show when it opened.

Opens   Closes

Minutes past 29

Write the time in words on the dotted
line underneath each clock.

Twenty minutes past seven

Forty minutes past three

Matching times 30

Each clock is being described by two mice. Draw
lines to join the correct two mice to each one.

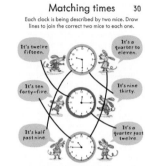

It's twelve fifteen.
It's a quarter to eleven.
It's ten forty-five.
It's nine thirty.
It's half past nine.
It's a quarter past twelve.

Minutes past 31

Write the time in words on the dotted
line underneath each clock.

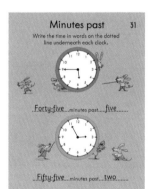

Forty-five minutes past five

Fifty-five minutes past two

Matching times 32

Each clock is being described by two mice. Draw
lines to join the correct two mice to each one.

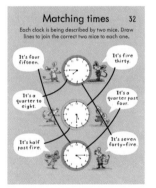

It's four fifteen.
It's five thirty.
It's a quarter to eight.
It's a quarter past four.
It's half past five.
It's seven forty-five.

Running late 33

These friends were due to meet for lunch at a
quarter past twelve. Draw the hands on the
clocks to show when each of them will arrive.

It's a quarter past twelve now. Where are the others?
Sorry, I'm going to be another twenty-five minutes.
I'll be there in fifteen minutes!
I'm five minutes away!

Arriving early 34

Art class starts at 1pm and these animals have
all arrived early. Draw the time on the clocks
to show when each of them arrived.

I'm ten minutes early.
I've already been here for ten minutes, Marvin.
Peck
Marvin
I got here five minutes before you, Peck.
You can all come in now!
Coly

Minutes past 35

Write the time in words on the dotted
line underneath each clock.

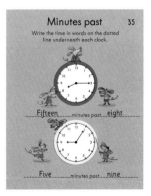

Fifteen minutes past eight

Five minutes past nine

What time is it? 36

Draw a line to join each animal to
the clock he or she is talking about.

It's twenty past ten.
It's ten to twelve.
It's five to four.

Answers

The circus is coming 37

Harley needs to put up posters the Saturday before the circus arrives. Draw a circle around the date he needs to put up posters.

A date to remember 38

Cody will arrange for the bunting to be taken down ten days after the circus leaves. Draw a triangle around the date Cody needs to remember.

Minutes past 39

Write the time in words on the dotted line underneath each clock.

Thirty-five minutes past six

Twenty-five minutes past three

What time is it? 40

Draw a line to join each animal to the clock he or she is talking about.

Peck's skating lesson 41

Peck's ice skating lesson is forty minutes long and starts at 9:45. Draw the hands on the clocks to show when his lesson starts and finishes.

Brenda's skating lesson 42

Brenda's ice skating lesson is fifty minutes long and starts at 10:20. Draw the hands on the clocks to show when her lesson starts and finishes.

Running late 43

These friends were supposed to meet for tea and cake at four twenty. Draw the hands on the clocks to show when each of them will arrive.

Arriving early 44

Writing class starts at 3:30pm and these animals have all arrived early. Draw the time on the clocks to show when each of them arrived.

Camping trip 45

The animals arrived at camp in the morning on the 11th of July, and leave in the evening on the 17th. Circle those dates on the calendar. Then, write the duration of the camping trip in days on the dotted line.

7 days

Answers

Lots of snow 46

It started to snow in the forest on the 23rd of January and stopped snowing the morning of the 30th. Circle those dates on the calendar, then write on the dotted line the length of time it snowed for in weeks.

1 week

Skateboarding 47

Draw the hands on the clocks to show the time the skateboarding competition starts and finishes.

Starts   Finishes

Football match 48

Draw the hands on the clocks to show when the football match starts and finishes.

Starts   Finishes

Plane to Mouse Island 49

Read the sign, then write on the dotted lines the time each plane will arrive at Mouse Island.

The Whistler   9.45am

Seadart   12.15pm

Captain Cloud   5pm

Return journey 50

Read the sign, then write on the dotted lines the time each plane will arrive at Cuthbert's Cliff.

The Whistler   11am

Seadart   2.30pm

Captain Cloud   6.15pm

Minutes past 51

Write the time in words on the dotted line underneath each clock.

forty-three minutes past one

four minutes past five

At the dentist 52

Suki needs to see the dentist. Her appointment is at two thirty. Show that time on the blank clock, then write on the dotted line the number of minutes she has to wait until her appointment.

28 minutes

Minutes past 53

Write the time in words on the dotted line underneath each clock.

twenty-eight minutes past twelve

fifty-six minutes past six

At the hairdresser 54

Peck's haircut is at twenty past eleven. Show that time on the blank clock, then write on the dotted line the number of minutes she has to wait until her appointment.

33 minutes

Answers

Minutes past 55

Write the time in words on the dotted line underneath each clock.

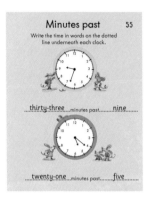

thirty-three minutes past nine

twenty-one minutes past five

The weather in March 56

Dilly's reading the weather forecast for March. Circle all the sunny days on the calendar. Now write on the dotted line the length of time it will be sunny for, in weeks and days.

From 12th March it will be sunny every day for ten days in a row.

1 week(s) and 3 days

Minutes past 57

Write the time in words on the dotted line underneath each clock.

fifty-eight minutes past twelve

eleven minutes past ten

The weather in April 58

Dilly's reading the weather forecast for April. Circle all the cloudy days on the calendar. Now write on the dotted line the length of time it will be cloudy for, in days.

From the 12th to the 27th we can expect solid cloud.

16 days

Waiting for the bus 59

The mice's bus is due at eight fifty-six. Show that time on the blank clock, then write on the dotted line the number of minutes the mice have to wait for their bus.

It won't be long now!

50 minutes

Waiting for the train 60

Cody's train has been delayed. It's now due at seven forty-two. Show that time on the blank clock, then write on the dotted line the number of minutes he has to wait until it arrives.

54 minutes

On the phone 61

Brenda called Bernie at five forty-five and they're still talking. Write on the dotted line the length of time they have been on the phone for.

And THEN what happened?

Oh Bernie, you should have seen it.

45 minutes

Windy days 62

This month these friends flew their kites every day from the 3rd to the 11th. Circle each day of kite-flying on the calendar, then write on the dotted line the number of weeks and days they flew their kites for.

1 week(s) and 2 days

Wrapping presents 63

Suki started wrapping presents at eight twenty-five. Write on the dotted line the number of minutes she has been wrapping presents for.

Marvin will love this.

52 minutes

Answers

Lots of rain 64
In February it rained every day from the 19th to the 28th. Circle those two dates on the calendar, then write on the dotted line the number of days it rained for.

10 days

What time is it? 65
Draw lines to join each analogue clock to the matching digital clock.

11 : 45

02 : 15

05 : 30

On the clock 66
Write the time on the dotted line next to each clock. One has been done for you.

04 : 30 — Half past four

10 : 15 — A quarter past ten

07 : 00 — Seven o'clock

12 : 45 — A quarter to one

What time is it? 67
Draw lines to join each digital clock to the matching analogue clock.

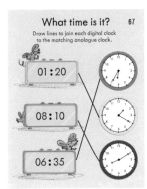

01 : 20

08 : 10

06 : 35

On the clock 68
Write the time on the dotted line next to each clock. One has been done for you.

02 : 40 — Twenty to three

12 : 05 — Five past twelve

05 : 45 — A quarter to six

11 : 10 — Ten past eleven

Marvin's train 69
This analogue clock shows the time now. Marvin's train will arrive soon. Write the 'pm' time on the digital display board to show when it will arrive.

1st. LONE TREE PLAIN
Calling at: Hopping Common, Fir View and Lone Tree Plain.

Arrives at 17 : 55

My train will arrive in fifteen minutes.

Departure times 70
Draw the hands on the analogue clocks to show when each animal's train will depart.

1st. Fir Town Calling at: Fir Town only.
2nd. Pine View Calling at: Cedar Grove and Pine View.
TIME NOW 12 : 10

My train departs in twelve minutes.

My train won't leave for another five minutes.

Kite flying 71
It's 16:30 and these friends started flying their kites forty-five minutes ago. Circle the clock that shows when they started.

15:30   15:45   15:05

Running 72
It's 11:05 and Harley and Cody started running forty minutes ago. Circle the clock that shows when they started running.

Can we stop now?

10:45   10:25   10:10

Answers

AM or PM? 73

Draw a circle around
each 'am' time below.

14:07 (05:11)

23:09 19:25

(10:43) 06:19

From earliest to latest 74

Draw arrows to join up these 'am' times
in order, starting with the earliest
and finishing with the latest.

11:30 07:55

05:20 10:35

10:50 09:40

AM or PM? 75

Draw a circle around
each 'pm' time below.

07:19 (20:54)

(17:09) (23:59)

00:04 11:16

From earliest to latest 76

Draw arrows to join up these 'pm'
times in order, starting with the
earliest and finishing with the latest.

15:15 13:46

16:04 23:32

18:00 19:57

Harley's day 77

Draw a line to join up Harley's day
in the correct order. Start with the
earliest time and finish with the latest.

12:40

11:00

15:50

09:25

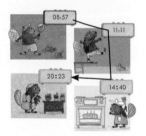

Bernie's day 78

Draw a line to join up Bernie's day in
the correct order. Start with the
earliest time and finish with the latest.

08:57

11:11

20:23

14:40

Story writing 79

It's the morning of the 8th of May and Harley is
writing a story for a magazine. He has ten days
left to finish it before the magazine is printed.
Draw a circle around the date it will be printed.

...and then
...a genie
appeared!

May

Mon	Tues	Wed	Thurs	Fri	Sat	Sun
29	30	1	2	3	4	5
6	7	8	9	10	11	12
13	14	15	16	17	(18)	19
20	21	22	23	24	25	26
27	28	29	30	31	1	2

Concert time 80

It's the 6th of October. Dilly and Bernie
cannot wait for the Super Skunks concert.
Circle the date of the concert on the calendar,
then write how many weeks are left to go.

SUPER
SKUNKS!
27th October

I ♥
SUPER
SKUNKS!

October

Mon	Tues	Wed	Thurs	Fri	Sat	Sun
31	1	2	3	4	5	6
7	8	9	10	11	12	13
14	15	16	17	18	19	20
21	22	23	24	25	26	(27)
28	29	30	31	1	2	3

......3......weeks

Basketball game 81

Marvin's basketball game started at 7pm.
Fill in the digital clocks to show
when the game started and finished.

That was such
a great game!

It was two
hours and fifteen
minutes, though.
Phew!

Started   Finished

19:00   21:15

Answers

Hours and minutes 82

The duration of each TV programme is given in minutes. Write the duration of each programme in hours and minutes on the dotted lines.

Channel 20
TREE RESCUE
12:30
102 minutes

1 hour and 42 minutes

Channel 3
Did You Know?
13:00
88 minutes

1 hour and 28 minutes

Time for a film 83

Suki's film is starting. It is 92 minutes long. Draw and write the time it will finish on the clocks below.

Two Flew into the Owls Nest

Start

16:10

Finish

17:42

Minutes only 84

The duration of each TV programme is given in hours and minutes. Write on the dotted lines the duration of each programme in minutes only.

Channel 6
Mouse Masterclass
14:30
1 hour and 15 minutes

75 minutes

Channel 43
Leaf Watch
18:10
1 hour and 55 minutes

115 minutes

What time is it? 85

Draw lines to join each analogue clock to the matching digital time.

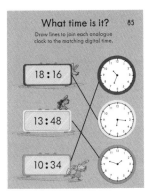

18:16

13:48

10:34

Years and months 86

These friends know how old their trees are in months only. Write on the dotted lines how old their trees are in years and months.

My tree is twenty-six months old

2 years and 2 months

My tree is fourteen months old

1 year and 2 months

Bus timetable 87

Dilly and Peck's bus departs at 15:40. On the timetable, draw a ring around the time they will arrive at Cabin Lodge.

I'm so tired from our hike.

We can put our feet up at Cabin Lodge!

Route 71 – Raccoon Ranch to Firtown						
	Monday–Saturday				Sundays	
Raccoon Ranch	0730	1120	1505	1542	1003	1749
Windy Creek		1155	1540	1617	1038	
Long River	0825	1215	1620	1737	1058	
Cabin Lodge		1307	1708	2025	1146	1909
Firtown	0845	1242	1713	2030	1151	1914

Journey duration 88

Complete the other side of this page. Now, write the duration of Dilly and Peck's bus journey on the dotted line in hours and minutes.

Ah, a nice cup of cocoa.

Zzzzzz

1 hour and 28 minutes

What time is it? 89

Draw lines to join each analogue clock to the matching digital time.

04:45

07:27

11:09

Months only 90

These friends know how old their trees are in years and months. Write on the dotted lines how old their trees are in months only.

My tree is three years and one month old

37 months old

My tree is one year and ten months old

22 months old

Answers

Brenda's train 91

This analogue clock shows the time now. Brenda's train will arrive soon. Write the 'pm' time on the digital display board to show when it will arrive.

1st. RACCOON RANCH
Calling at: Windy Creek, and Raccoon Ranch.

Arrives at ...12 : 25...

I've got ten minutes until my train arrives.

Departure times 92

Draw the hands on the analogue clocks to show when each animal's train will depart.

1st. Windy Creek *Calling at: Hawthorn Hill and Windy Creek.*
2nd. Long River *Calling at: Long River only.*
TIME NOW 17 : 50

My train departs in twelve minutes.

My train won't leave for another five minutes.

Matching times 93

The animals know the duration of their journeys. Draw a line to match each animal to the correct departure board.

My journey will be an hour and five minutes.

My journey will be seventeen minutes.

My journey will be fifty-five minutes.

FIRTOWN
Departs at 07:19
Arrives at 07:36

CABIN LODGE
Departs at 16:02
Arrives at 16:57

LONG RIVER
Departs at 13:15
Arrives at 14:20

Dilly's baking 94

Help Dilly follow her cake recipe this afternoon. Look at the analogue clock, then write the time on the digital clock after each step.

Step 1. Mix the ingredients together for ten minutes.

15 : 40

Step 2. Pour the mixture into a cake tin and bake in the oven for twenty minutes.

16 : 00

Step 3. Take out the cake and leave to cool for fifteen minutes.

16 : 15

Bernie's baking 95

Bernie is making a flan for lunch. Look at the analogue clock, then write the time on the digital clock after each step.

Step 1. Roll out a circle of pastry and place in a flan tin. This will only take five minutes.

11 : 50

Step 2. Mix the ingredients together for ten minutes until smooth.

12 : 00

Step 3. Pour the mixture over the pastry and bake in the oven for twenty-five minutes.

12 : 25

Matching times 96

The animals know the duration of their journeys. Draw a line to match each animal to the correct train.

FIR VIEW
Departs at 11:15
Arrives at 13:45

WINDY CREEK
Departs at 15:25
Arrives at 15:50

RACCOON RANCH
Departs at 09:15
Arrives at 10:35

My journey will be an hour and twenty minutes.

My journey will be twenty-five minutes.

My journey will be two and a half hours.

Bus timetable 97

It's four o'clock on Tuesday and Suki and Cody need to be in Firtown by 6pm for Brenda's party. Draw a ring around the time they need to get the bus.

I hope we get there in time for the party.

Route 71 – Raccoon Ranch to Firtown					
	Monday–Saturday				Sundays
Raccoon Ranch	0730	1120	1505	1542	1003	1749
Windy Creek		1155	1540	1617	1038	
Long River	0825	1215	1620	1737	1058	
Cabin Lodge		1307	1708	2025	1146	1909
Firtown	0845	1242	1713	2030	1151	1914

Journey duration 98

Complete the other side of this page. Now, write the duration of Cody and Suki's bus journey on the dotted line.

I think Brenda likes her present...

Happy birthday, Brenda!

...53 minutes...

Path laying 99

It's the 2nd of October. Harley and Suki are laying a new path in the park. It needs to be finished in three weeks. Draw a circle around the deadline date.

We need to finish the path in time for the music festival!

October						
Mon	Tues	Wed	Thurs	Fri	Sat	Sun
30	1	2	3	4	5	6
7	8	9	10	11	12	13
14	15	16	17	18	19	20
21	22	23	24	25	26	27
28	29	30	31	1	2	3

Answers

Holiday time 100

It's the 15th of August. Dilly is going on holiday in four days' time and needs to pack. Draw a circle around the date she goes on holiday.

Oh I can't decide!

August
Mon	Tue	Wed	Thurs	Fri	Sat	Sun
29	30	31	1	2	3	4
5	6	7	8	9	10	11
12	13	14	15	16	17	18
(19)	20	21	22	23	24	25
26	27	28	29	30	31	1

TV schedule 101

How long is each TV programme? Draw lines to join up the programmes with their descriptions.

Forest Falls
18:15 — 18:45

The High Life
20:05 — 21:35

WOODLANDERS
21:00 — 21:40

An hour and a half of non-stop action. Don't miss it!

You'll be gripped by this fast-paced drama series; each episode is only 40 minutes.

Prepare for giggles galore in this half hour special from your favourite comedian.

Skating festival 102

It's the ice skating festival today. Write the duration of each event on the dotted lines.

Speed skating competition
13:20 – 13:50

__30 minutes__

Partner dancing
14:05 – 14:35

__30 minutes__

Freestyle skate
15:10 – 15:30

__20 minutes__

Film times 103

Draw arrows to join up the starting times of the films in the correct order. Start with the earliest time and finish with the latest.

Ballet Bears	08:20	13:00
Moose on the Loose	14:05	18:30
Autumn Days	10:45	11:30
River Rescue: Part 2	16:10	19:55

Film duration 104

Draw a line to join up the durations of the animals' films in the correct order. Start with the shortest film and finish with the longest.

My film was two hours.

My film was an hour and twenty minutes.

My film was an hour and ten minutes.

My film was 70 minutes.

Film times 105

Draw arrows to join up the starting times of the films in the correct order. Start with the earliest time and finish with the latest.

Armadillo in New York	12:05	21:40
Broken Branches	11:10	13:35
The Quiet Road	13:25	20:50
The Secret Forest	09:30	15:00

Film duration 106

Draw a line to join up the durations of the animals' films in the correct order. Start with the longest film and finish with the shortest.

My film was 70 minutes.

My film was an hour and a half.

My film was only an hour.

My film was nearly three hours!

TV schedule 107

How long is each TV programme? Draw lines to join up the programmes with their descriptions.

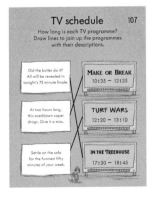

Did the butler do it? All will be revealed in tonight's 75 minute finale.

At two hours long, this overblown caper drags. Give it a miss.

Settle on the sofa for the funniest fifty minutes of your week.

MAKE OR BREAK
10:35 – 12:35

TURF WARS
12:20 – 13:10

IN THE TREEHOUSE
17:30 – 18:45

Swimming gala 108

It's the swimming gala today. Write the duration of each event on the dotted lines.

100 METRES FRONT CRAWL
09:40 – 09:50

__10 minutes__

TREADING WATER
10:15 – 10:20

__5 minutes__

HIGH DIVE
11:45 – 12:10

__25 minutes__

Answers

Hours and minutes   109

These friends have spent 80 minutes fishing. Write on the dotted line the length of time they have been fishing for in hours and minutes.

I've found some tiny fish!

I can see a few more, Marvin.

1 hour and 20 minutes

Matching times   110

Draw a line to match up each pair of animals who are talking about the same length of time.

I've got twenty minutes to read my script.

I've got thirty minutes until the play starts.

I need to be ready in fifteen minutes!

I've got five minutes longer than you.

The play starts in half an hour.

I've only got half that time to get ready!

Minutes only   111

The Super Skunks have been playing for three hours and seven minutes. Write on the dotted line the length of time they have been playing for in minutes only.

Whoop whoop!

They're great!

I ♥ SUPER SKUNKS

187 minutes

Matching times   112

Draw a line to match up each pair of animals who are talking about the same length of time.

My dental appointment is in ten minutes.

I've been waiting twice that long!

Phew, twenty minutes – that wasn't too long.

Don't eat or drink for a quarter of an hour.

I've been here for fifteen minutes.

I've been here five minutes less than that.

Years and months   113

These friends know how old their trees are in months only. Write on the dotted lines how old their trees are in years and months.

My tree is twenty eight months old.

2 years and 4 months

My tree is seventeen months old.

1 year and 5 months

Months only   114

These friends know how old their trees are in years and months. Write on the dotted lines how old their trees are in months only.

My tree is a year and nine months old.

21 months old

My tree is just a year old.

12 months old

Film times   115

Draw arrows to join up the starting times of these films in the correct order. Start with the earliest time and finish with the latest.

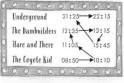

Underground	21:25 → 22:15
The Dambuilders	12:35 → 13:15
Hare and There	11:05 15:45
The Coyote Kid	08:50 → 10:10

Film duration   116

Draw a line to join up the durations of the animals' films in the correct order. Start with the shortest film and finish with the longest.

My film was 100 minutes long.

Mine was half as long as that.

My film was an hour and a half.

Mine was twice as long as yours!

Dilly's baking   117

Dilly is making a cake again this afternoon. Look at the analogue clock, then write the time on the digital clock after each step of the recipe.

Step 1. Mix the ingredients together for fifteen minutes.

13 : 00

Step 2. Pour the mixture into a cake tin and bake in the oven for thirty-five minutes.

13 : 35

Step 3. Take out the out and leave to cool for twenty minutes.

13 : 55

Answers

Bernie's baking 118

Bernie is making a pie this morning. Look at the analogue clock, then write the time on the digital clock after each step of the recipe.

Step 1. Roll out two pastry circles and place one in a pie dish. This will take ten minutes.

10 : 35

Step 2. Make the pie filling and put in the pie dish. This will take twenty-five minutes.

11 : 00

Step 3. Put the second pastry circle on top and bake in the oven for thirty minutes.

11 : 30

Matching times 119

Each clock is being described by two mice. Draw lines to join the correct two mice to each one.

It's five fifteen.
It's seven minutes to five.
It's four fifty-three.
It's a quarter to two.
It's one forty-five.
It's a quarter past five.

17:15
13:45
04:53

Dilly's bus 120

Dilly is waiting for a bus. She is due to arrive in Firtown at a quarter to nine. Draw a ring around the time of the bus she is waiting for.

Where is the bus?

Route 71 – Raccoon Ranch to Firtown					
	Monday–Saturday			Sundays	
Raccoon Ranch	0730	1120	1505	1542	1003	1749
Windy Creek		1155	1540	1617	1038	
Long River	0825	1215	1620	1737	1058	
Cabin Lodge		1307	1708	2025	1146	1909
Firtown	0845	1242	1713	2030	1151	1914

Marvin's bus 121

It's three o'clock on Friday and Marvin wants to get to Long River before the shops close at half past five. Draw a ring around the time he needs to get the bus.

I need a new hat!

Route 71 – Raccoon Ranch to Firtown					
	Monday–Saturday			Sundays	
Raccoon Ranch	0730	1120	1505	1542	1003	1749
Windy Creek		1155	1540	1617	1038	
Long River	0825	1215	1620	1737	1058	
Cabin Lodge		1307	1708	2025	1146	1909
Firtown	0845	1242	1713	2030	1151	1914

Matching times 122

Each clock is being described by two mice. Draw lines to join the correct two mice to each one.

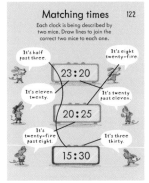

It's half past three.
It's eight twenty-five.
It's eleven twenty.
It's twenty past eleven.
It's twenty-five past eight.
It's three thirty.

23:20
20:25
15:30

The pirate play 123

The pirate play is starting. The interval will be at eight fifteen. Show that time on the blank clock, then write on the dotted line how long it is until the interval.

19 : 35   20 : 15

Sail Away!
by Marvin

Captain Bessie
played by Brenda

Despicable Sue
played by Dilly

Pirate Paul
played by Bernie

40 minutes

Interval 124

The interval is over and the play is about to start again. It will finish at nine thirty. Show that time on the blank clock, then write on the dotted line how long it is until the play finishes.

20 : 25   21 : 30

Sail Away!
by Marvin

Pirate Joe
played by Cody

Sailor Sol
played by Suki

Pirate Pete
played by Peck

65 minutes

A rainy day 125

It's due to stop raining today at 2pm. Write that time on the blank clock, then write on the dotted lines the number of hours and minutes Brenda and Bernie have to wait until it stops raining.

11 : 50   14 : 00

2 hours and 10 minutes.

Waiting for the ferry 126

Brenda and Bernie's ferry is delayed until five past five. Write on the dotted line the number of minutes Brenda and Bernie will have to wait for their ferry.

16 : 24

41 minutes

Answers

Hours and minutes 127

The duration of each TV programme is given in minutes. Write on the dotted lines the duration of each programme in hours and minutes.

Channel 17
TREASURE HUNT
193 minutes

3 hours and 13 minutes

Channel 2
SING WITH SUKI
65 minutes

1 hour and 5 minutes

Minutes only 128

The duration of each TV programme is given in hours and minutes. Write on the dotted lines the duration of each programme in minutes only.

Channel 23
DO IT YOURSELF
2 hours and 10 minutes

130 minutes

Channel 30
CAR CHAT
1 hour and 40 minutes

100 minutes

Stopwatch times 129

These animals have completed their sports day races in less than an hour. Write their times on the blank stopwatches below.

We finished in twenty minutes and twenty-six seconds.

I finished in fifty eight seconds!

00 : 20 : 26   00 : 00 : 58

Ordering results 130

These animals have finished the morning fun run. Write in the boxes the order the animals finished the fun run in, from 1st to 4th.

00 : 46 : 10   2nd

01 : 30 : 57   3rd

01 : 57 : 35   4th

00 : 23 : 06   1st

Timing 131

Suki is timing Brenda doing her homework. Write her time on the blank stopwatch below.

02 : 09 : 33

You've been going for two hours, nine minutes and thirty three seconds, Brenda, keep it up!

Ordering results 132

These animals have finished the afternoon fun run. Write in the boxes the order the animals finished the fun run in, from 1st to 4th.

02 : 31 : 45   4th

02 : 17 : 03   3rd

01 : 08 : 29   1st

01 : 48 : 45   2nd

Stopwatch times 133

These animals have completed their sports day races. Write their times on the blank stopwatches below.

I finished in seven minutes and seventeen seconds.

We finished in eleven minutes and thirty nine seconds.

00 : 07 : 17   00 : 11 : 39

Timing 134

Suki is timing how long Harley can keep his kite in the air for. Write his time so far on the blank stopwatch below.

It's been twelve minutes and five seconds.

00 : 12 : 05

Timing 135

It's a stormy day and Suki is timing how long it is after seeing the lightning that she and Dilly hear the thunderclap. Write the time they have recorded on the blank stopwatch below.

So that was sixteen seconds.

There's the rumble!

00 : 00 : 16